Kay Freeman spent most of her life in higher education, as a scholar who transitioned to helping other scholars realize their educational quest. She is a daughter, whose parents died when she was just starting her adult life, but they were so proud of all of her achievements, tenacity for success, and zest for life. Her only sister passed away from a brain tumor five weeks after her diagnosis. This book is dedicated to her sister, as she embraced life and was Kay's true friend and biggest supporter. Her sister's last words to Kay was for her to "live her life", and that is what Kay is doing each and every day.

I dedicate this book to my sister, Donna, and my family for their love and strength through my ordeal. I convey my hearth felt gratitude to all those cancer survivors who kept me in their prayers and showered me with their guidance. I thank my entire medical team for their dedication, knowledge, and compassion. I also thank my colleagues from CASL and Fielding Graduate University for their support and love during my ordeal.

Kay Freeman

12 DAYS OF CANCER

From Patton Leather Shoes to Pearls

AUSTIN MACAULEY PUBLISHERS™

LONDON · CAMBRIDGE · NEW YORK · SHARJAH

Ordering Information
Quantity sales: Special discounts are available on quantity purchases by corporations, associations, and others. For details, contact the publisher at the address below.

Publisher's Cataloguing-in-Publication data
Freeman, Kay
12 Days of Cancer

ISBN 9781638299455 (Paperback)
ISBN 9781638299462 (Hardback)
ISBN 9781638299479 (ePub e-book)

Library of Congress Control Number: 2022919875

www.austinmacauley.com/us

First Published 2023
Austin Macauley Publishers LLC
40 Wall Street,33rd Floor, Suite 3302
New York, NY 10005
USA

mail-usa@austinmacauley.com
+1 (646) 5125767

To my Papa, whose love, advice, and support gave me the will to stay strong and to assume most roles assigned to me. Thank you for not leaving me alone on this road and others!

I would like to thank my supervisor Dr. Orlando Taylor for inspiring me to reach for the top shelf. His wisdom and guidance helped me through my battle.

Table of Contents

From Patton Leather to Pearls

Chapter 1
A Letter to My Cancer
Co-Survivors

Dear Jay, Jayden, Shadow, and Eliza:

I know this is a frightening time filled with uncertainty and most of all a haunting of déjà vu. We have endured so many family losses, a decade of deaths consisting of in-laws (grandparents) and Aunt Donna which was the hardest death. Now, you are faced with the possibility of my demise and how do you digest this as a reality, what do you make of it and how do you fix it? Maybe this is a misdiagnosis or perhaps it's my time to be next. How does a mother say, "Goodbye?" How does a wife tell her best friend who she has known for more than half her life on this earth, "You must be strong, walk the rest of this road without me and take care of our kids as we intended." Cancer is scary and ultimately carries an off-melody tune of pain with a looming question of will death become me from this disease? Well, I never accepted the conclusion of death because I am a fighter who does not capitulate.

But cancer will take you to a dark and painful place via treatments. You will lose your independence from weight loss and will find yourself clutching to the banister when you try to walk up the stairs praying you will not endure a spasm. You plot your chemo path by preparing in advance with your Vera Bradley bag packed with the necessities for uncertainty. Necessities – what if I spew all over myself during treatment or what if I can't make it to the ladies' room in time. You are being infused with a copious amount of liquid along with your consumption of a liter of water, as you know the next step is to release all of those liquids while you are tired, weak, and dazed. You sit in the chemo chair pretending all is well and I am going to beat cancer, and you will but living in the moment your body is being filled with toxins which are supposed to eradicate the cancer cells and all other cells as well. This was my journey, feeling weak, tired, and sick from chemo but then pretending I was not in pain, trying to maintain the outer appearance of sophistication with a bald head. One day after my sixth chemo treatment, I looked in the mirror and saw my eyebrows and lashes gone that is when I knew I had to fight much harder.

Jayden and Shadow, you made me strong, you challenged my will with your love and words which impacted my heart. If it were not for the two of you, my extra charge of the fight might have dwindled.

Eliza, your tough girl exterior and trying to live up to the daughter you think you should be is not working auspiciously; instead, be you, "The girl that chose me to be your mom," as you once said. You know what that phrase means, so find your way back to being "Bella, and Lil Girl!"

Jay, your love and support made me angry. Yes, angry! Because I know how much you truly love and depend on me; thereby, how could I trust you will take care of our kids as we intended? You would have to go on with life as if I mattered minimally. You would have to devote your life, time, and heart to raising our children and to transforming into both mom and dad. You are unable to do this without me because your special touches are gender-biased filled with extreme love or all of nothing, and let the chips fall where they may. Together, we are a powerful team. Singularly, there are noticeable deficits. If I had to be both mom and dad, our kids would be overly successful with no clue of how to relax and enjoy life. Their happiness would be built around their success; instead of evenly devoted to a balanced life. My statement of how I think you would raise our kids is not meant to be judgmental or acrimonious as you know I am bluntly honest. Rather, it is meant to convey I know the sadness you will feel in your heart; thereby, not allowing yourself to enjoy our kids' growth without me. You are truly a good man who made me not only know the definition of happiness but filled my life with joy and laughter; thereby, as a unit, our kids know the totality of a balanced and successful life. As a singular, they will only know our strengths and apprehensions. Raising our kids alone for you would be filled with sadness because I remember the boy I met when his father died, you were so sad not allowing yourself to be happy and most of all not allowing anyone to get close to you. Your wall was high and made of concrete which I guess is a good match for my brick wall!

Hence, I cannot die I want to raise my kids and be there to laugh at my husband's jokes. Is it my choice to live or does a higher being make this decision? I have prayed for everyone and everything in my life but never for my own life, so I asked God to spare my life because I want to enjoy the four blessings that he provided to me after calling my parents, uncle, and sister home. They say you are never given more than you can handle, but it is accentuated that you are blessed with all that you deserve. I never placed work ahead of my family, I just wanted to be able to provide for my kids and to be an equal partner. You and I always embraced the future of our kids growing to maturity and financial independence so that we can go off and finish discovering America and elsewhere. I am not remorseful that I never backpack through Europe as a young girl because I knew I wanted to do that with you as we move into the next phase of our lives.

If you are a co-survivor, your strength, determination, love, and patience are needed. Do not pull away nor stop talking, believe me, your conveyance of normalcy and continuation of life is what motivates us to stay hopeful and positive for survival. I do not intend to live my life in an hourglass, holding my breath each time I go for a scan, etc.; instead, I am taking charge of my life and showing God how grateful I am to be alive so that the extension of my life is inevitable.

Chapter 2
12 Days of Cancer

I never thought in a million years I would be diagnosed with cancer, nor did I think the pattern of this disease would spiral into an unbelievable path. I felt an indention on my left breast which I attributed to my wire bra and/or the lifting of my carry-on that pressed against my chest. Of course, I discounted this indention and believed it would disappear, after all, it was not painful or deformed in any way just a little bump. I was so busy with life and work which I know many of you can identify.

Friday, February 14, 2020, Valentine's Day – During my routine exam with my doctor, as I was about to get dress and she was typing in her notes, I casually mentioned this indention. Not sure why I remembered to do this, but after my story, you will see this act saved my life! She looked at the indention and said, "There is no evidence of a mass, your mammograms are negative and I do suspect it is trauma." Thank goodness, she is a professional who puts her patients first and does not discount what may be. She ordered a mammogram just so that we can discount any possibility of the improbable and ascertain what may be occurring.

Monday, February 17, President's Day – I went into the facility with no worries or concern, after all, breast cancer is not a probability for me, no family history of it, or any traces of concern from what I researched, meaning no mass, drainage, deformity, etc. During the mammogram, a suspicious tiny nodule appeared in the indented area, so I was escorted into another room for a sonogram, the technician stated there is a nodule which is a bit suspicious. The doctor came in and looked at the monitor, explaining to me there is a suspicious nodule. He indicated the report will be sent to my doctor and she will either prescribe a biopsy or move in a different direction. In essence, the attitude of all parties was mellow as it was a nodule or something of suspicion not large enough to think of it as a mass. I never thought it could be cancer. Of course, I reached out to the Cancer Center for a conversation and to edify my knowledge of what this may be. I was told nodules can be cancerous and they can be benign. Just go through the process, stay positive, and take it one day at a time. This advice from the unknown voice on the other line turned out to be what helped me through the minutes, hours, days, and months to come.

Friday, February 21, 2020, Kay's Biopsy Day – This day was not a holiday, just another Friday with an invasive procedure that would remove small extraction of fluid, tissue to discern the intent of the suspicious nodule. I recollect the two technicians and the doctor who began to closely look at what may be nothing, life-changing or my death sentence. I am an inquisitive person who likes to know what is going on, as well as, the level of competency of the individuals who are seeking an answer to my nodule conundrum. They were all very competent with years of experience so, in my mind, I knew their attitude, body language, and verbal recitation during the performance of the procedure would be an indicator of whether I should be worried, or continue with my mellow attitude. The doctor conveyed to me there were three nodules, two of them were close in proximity at the 4 and 6 o'clock position, somewhat connecting, then there is a tiny 8 o'clock nodule that appears to be just forming.

In my mind, the doctor's recitation of the nodules did not prompt a major concern. Two nodules were close in proximity at 2 cm, the third nodule was in the forming stage. I was not worried, I felt in my heart these nodules were just benign and will be removed. So, I will continue with my busy life, overachieving; never taking breaks, always reaching for the basket filled with to-dos.

Wednesday, February 26, 2020, Anniversary of the day I met my husband – I received a call from the doctor who performed the biopsy at 2:30ish pm conveying I have cancer. Her voice and conveyance were incredulous to me and I could not believe what she was saying. As anyone would do in my position, I immediately called my attending physician who held my hand through the twelve days of fact-finding procedures. I needed to hear this diagnosis from her. The biopsy doctor does not know me, she is not equipped in my mind to convey something I never thought could be cancer. I was flustered, unhinged, and perplexed about what I should do next. Should I start researching options, begin reading every book on the subject, or just sit quietly thinking this cannot be an accurate finding. My attending physician was not in the office, so I spoke with another doctor in the practice. Even though the doctor within the practice confirmed the diagnosis, I still needed to hear it from my doctor. My trust in her coupled with her compassion for her patients, is the voice that I need to confirm, deny, or provide instruction for the next step, etc. My doctor called me the very next day, apologizing for not being the one to convey my result; of course, I was not in the mindset of feeling negativity toward the confirmation of my diagnosis. I just needed to hear it conveyed soothingly, with factual data and a tone of positivity.

My doctor confirmed there is cancer in the two nodules. The conveyance of bad news is arduous by itself, but oftentimes, if delivered by the right person whose tone is not filled with despair, hopelessness, or emptiness, the recipient of the news may find peace and strength to move on to the next step. Fortunately, for me my physician was that person, she provided contacts for further exploration and next steps. Well, there you have it my twelve days of cancer! A definitive diagnosis on the day I cherished so very much because it was the beginning of a life I dreamed of. On February 26, I met the guy who later became my husband and now my co-survivor. How do I tell him of my diagnosis? How do I tell him the day, he proclaimed was the start of his life when he met me, is the very same day decades later, I am diagnosed with a deadly disease that may end our union or at least, test the parts in our wedding vows?

Did I cry on the 12th day of cancer? No, I was in a mood of silence and acceptance, why I do not know, maybe I was numb or as described the girl who sees a bouquet in the desert? Yes, I am an optimist, but now I have to find a way to feel positivity for myself with faith for an auspicious outcome. My diagnosis was followed by the collection of fact-finding data to prognosticate the treatment level, stage of cancer, and outcome. Oh, did I neglect to mention we were in the height of the COVID pandemic, which required us to be in isolation at home, wearing a mask when in public, staying six feet apart from each other, and constantly washing our hands or using hand sanitizer until we could wash our hands? Yes, in addition to having cancer I need to ensure I do not contract COVID which does carry the probability of life finality.

Chapter 3
Stepping Back, Who Am I?

I always prided myself on being a mom and wife first then an employee who has to endure all of life's challenges. I am small with curly black hair which I attribute to receiving from my father. My parents died at the start of my adulthood. I believe we have to undergo a series of steps or progressions through life which begins at infancy to maturity. My start of adulthood began a few years after graduating from college as I ventured out on my own, going from my parents' home to my husband's home and working at a job in higher education that would soon become an unintended career. I never really lived an independent life; I went from one abode to the next. So, I don't know how to wake up to silence and lounge about in my favorite pajamas, sitting on a corner of the sofa watching mindless sitcoms or never-ending Hallmark Christmas movies.

I don't regret my life as I think it progressed as it should have, now if given a second chance to issue alterations, of course, I would do just that. Meaning, I would live a cavalier life-embracing an existence free or controlled of stress in both mind and body. This type of life is possible, although we think it is not. Living in a high-producing life filled with stress and always trying to be the best is tiresome, and believe me, it does not have an ending point or peak, rather it is infinite. The death of my parents was the beginning of my maturity level as I accepted the harshness of life; I never thought I would be no one's child.

I made a promise not to inflict the pain of uncertainty and instability of death on my children. I never really lived my life, I did as I was told, always walk on the right side of the road never taking a risk that would result in an inauspicious outcome. I tried to be the best mom and wife I could be. In essence, I am from an era of perfection, reach for it, emulate it, and if you do not have it within your portfolio, ask yourself why. So, now that I am faced with cancer and am not equipped to fix this issue, what do I do? I am a fixer so I have been referred to when recruited from one job to the next. My current supervisor once said to me folks have taken advantage of me. I did not agree with that statement until I walked the cancer road. When I conveyed to my supervisor I was diagnosed with cancer, he replied reassuringly, you are not alone, I will walk this road with you. I never heard such words of love and compassion from my employers as they only wanted me to place them on the extol platform resulting from my work. He kept his word and did walk the cancer road with me. If I did not maintain the modified employment schedule, I would not have been able to hold on to the possibility of resuming back to my life or the normalcy of my life. I never imagined I would be blessed to work among individuals who truly know the meaning of the words humanity and compassion.

Now that I can visually see who I was through my lens, I can honestly say, when I looked at a photo of myself a year ago, I felt a prodigious amount of sadness. The girl in the photo was so sweet and so many people took advantage of her; never viewing her as a human being that deserved respect. Rather, they viewed her as someone whose position in life is to place them in the royal chair with the brightest spotlight; hence, my supervisor was correct! What do I say to that expectation; think again! I am no one's lackey, nor is my work subjected to being taken hostage and masqueraded as that of someone else. We allow people to treat us as they wish, we allow and accept inequality by masking it as an unintentional infliction which we must endure to get ahead, not so!

Chapter 4
Path One Planning,
Preparation, and Treatment

Now that I am diagnosed with cancer, the next step is to seek the medical attention necessary. I reached out to my primary physician, Dr. M, from this point I will use the first letter of my medical team. Yes, a team was assembled not by my request but that of a higher being, in my opinion. My visit to Dr. M was soon after my diagnosis, his response to me was the fuel I needed for my journey. He stated we will beat this, no time can be wasted, and this cancer of yours is aggressive, he further indicated he will walk this road with me. I could not believe my ears again, when and where is this army being assembled? Was it when I asked God to spare my life and help me through this diagnosis or was it when I said to God, "I will not be beaten by cancer."

During the information or data collection resulting from various tests, MRI, CT scan, genetic testing, etc. as to the severity of my nodules or what the next treatment level should be, the findings resulted as follows; no evidence of cancer in my lymph nodes, cancer is within the two nodules and appears to be 2 cm. In essence, my condition was not severe but did warrant surgery and radiation. During the cancer fact-finding, life was still progressing for me as I was offered, out of nowhere, an opportunity to interview for a vice president position at an institution I truly wanted to be affiliated with. Naturally, I thought this is crazy. Where is this opportunity coming from, and why now? I was not seeking employment outside of my current employer and my new title. This opportunity was a result of my former professional life which was infused with surreptitious recruitment from employers in need of enrollment development. Many of my opportunities were based on referrals from individuals who were familiar with my work. I thought, *What is this, a cruel joke or a way for me to run and escape the cancer road ahead of me.*

I recall conveying to my doctors the irony of this opportunity in a facetious manner. I could not believe my ears when my primary doctor, Dr. M, and my oncologist, Dr. F both indicated I should go for it, i.e., attend the interview. I thought attending the interview was insane and a bit deceptive on my behalf as I thought I was broken. Remember, I am from the world of perfect little girls who sit up straight, twirl like a ballerina, and never let them see you cry out loud. Dr. F conveyed to me based on the test results my cancer is a stage 0 and very curable with minimal next step treatments, so the possibility of me moving forward with a new career or whatever is possible.

I never realized the true intent of this unexpected interview, for it was a diversion of a blessing which I held on to during my cancer road walk. The interview lasted for an hour and a half and within that time, I was an intelligent, accomplished female being sought after for my record-breaking skillset and not a cancer patient. It felt great to be in control and not feel helpless to a malady of uncertainty that has taken the lives of so many. From the test results, and meeting with my surgeon, Dr. H, it appeared as though I was on my way to healing and recovery.

I underwent surgery on April 3, 2020, the day before my brother's birthday, and during the height of the COVID pandemic. No loved ones to accompany me beyond the entry point of Johns Hopkins Hospital; thereby, I walked down the lighted corridors to prepare for surgery only with the limited hospital personnel. It felt like a deserted hospital in one of those scary movies. I recall feeling anxious but positive. I had to endure some kind of wire inserted into my body for surgical purposes, that was not a nice feeling! I recall the hospital personnel trying to reassure me all will be well, but I could sense an undertone of fear from each of them as it relates to COVID. Needless to say, normalcy was not on the menu for that day. My surgery was completed and I was in recovery, my attending nurse wanted to exit the hospital as quickly as she entered, she did not want to stay beyond her work hour with a slow recovering patient. I cannot recall waking up on my own as I do not believe I did so, but who knows. All I remember is a medical attendee holding me up and saying I need to drink some fluid and get dressed so that I can stand. Well, that is not possible, as part of my body was sliced and diced, so I think I am entitled to at least a few minutes to collect myself. Instead of approaching this situation with anger, I asked the nurse to slow down, conveyed my gratitude to her for her bravery to report to work and help a stranger. Then I reassured her she is equipped for COVID because of her training and I need her help because I am battling the uncertainty of cancer. She immediately set aside her feelings of uneasiness and focused on me. Helping me to get dress, hold on to my dignity, and reassuring me the first step to my battle went well. I was so grateful to her and the entire hospital staff. People were dying from COVID and this was a real-life demon inflicting its venom in anyone as there was no restriction or privilege of exemption.

Sadly, to say when I was first diagnosed with cancer, the fear from my younger brother protruded with an unnecessary tantrum and directive to me of this is my last step as death is coming for me. I suppose each individual handles death and the possibility in a different form, I am not angry with him., but was disappointed as to the lack of his strength, which I realized, was not lacking but instead was evoked and provoked to convey information that I needed through this journey. Yes, had my cancer not been detected when it was, death was coming for me as I would have probably ended up in hospice with my husband and kids, crying in disbelief and agonizing pain. I know my husband would have tried to engage in some bargain with God to take him and spare me. My brother did and I thought that was sheer nonsense until I looked at the bigger picture and realized his love for me was unconditional. You see that kind of love on television, but never thinking it could be real or applicable to me.

As I am wheeled out of the hospital to meet my husband in the car, the very first statement out of my mouth while still being sedated was, "Well, I see I am not dead yet as forecasted by my brother." There was an uncomfortable silence as my husband was elated, I am sitting beside him and not otherwise, but in some small way, he did not know how to respond to my comment so he opted for silence. I took a deep breath and said, "Wow, did I just say that after surgery?"

He then exclaimed, "Yes, you did."

I cogitated for a minute and exclaimed, "Well, it's true, I am tough, and a wise man said a while ago, 'You will not be beaten.'"

So, I played that card of strength infused with sarcasm and maybe a dash of disappointing anger toward my brother. I expected him to be as strong as I and to show it in the same manner not realizing his strength is quiet like our father.

Chapter 5
Pathology Report
Not as Expected

About a week or so after surgery, the pathology report made its way to my patient portal. I opened the report and began to read it. After all, how complicated can it be?

I am educated but am I strong enough to decipher the language of ambiguity and definitiveness regarding my condition? The answer is "No." How can you read a report which states your condition is not a stage 0? The results of the biopsy from the specimen or tissues required two expert eyes and not one because the results were not as predicted from any of the data collected from my earlier test results. I kept re-reading the report and of course, I sent a copy to Dr. F. He called me and conveyed the report is "Not as expected." I asked him to simplify the conversation because I am not feeling confident. He explained 4 out of 4 lymph nodes were infected with cancer, cancer remains in the margins of my breast, and last but not least, my cancer is aggressive.

With this new development and concrete findings, immediate treatment needs to occur to desist cancer from spreading. I recall Dr. F and Dr. H speaking on the cell phone during my post-op appointment on April 20, 2020. Dr. H wanted me to immediately undergo surgery for full removal of my left breast; whereupon, Dr. F stated that would not be the best avenue to take since the cancer is spreading and progressing. He wanted me to undergo the strongest dosages of chemo for four months, then we can proceed with another surgery. On April 24, 2020, my wedding anniversary, I was meeting with Dr. F who informed me I will be undergoing minor surgery for a chemo port to be installed in the upper right part of my chest. This makes the chemo procedure or access easier. The following Monday, and another COVID medical environment left me in the surgery prep room alone without my husband who, by the way, was still waiting in our car in the parking lot for me. My only company in the surgical room were two nurses whose compassion outweighed their experience level; between the two of them, they had 60 plus years of nursing experience. There was an issue in drawing my blood, my body was still recuperating from surgery, my mind was in mental shock amalgamated with fear, uncertainty, and let us not forget, strong girl syndrome. Needless to say, it was a lot for me to digest and now you want blood. The nurse explained to me the installation of the chemo port cannot occur without the necessary blood work and from what she has read, I am scheduled to start chemo that Friday, May 1, 2020.

I recall all of the uncomfortable medical procedures which were only made more uncomfortable by COVID's requirement of spatial distancing, masked, and constant washing of the hands or using hand sanitizer. To have your loved one in the room with you or to hold the hand of strength from your spouse was not an option for me, so I not only faced cancer with uncertainty but I was alone. Surprisingly, the nurse who tried to take my blood the first time sensed my pain, and out of nowhere, she touched my hand with a gentle rub where the blood was to be drawn and she said, "Relax, my colleague will be very gentle in drawing your blood and all will be well." Then she stated, "Not to worry, I am here to help you and will not leave your side. You can do this!" Of course, the inner strength burst out and my blood was drawn successfully! I truly believe the compassion through touch helped me to relax with focused breathing which definitely prompted blood flow.

Entering the operating room, I see at least three doctors, needless to say, I am worried. I know I am not royalty, so why so many attending surgeons. I asked and they replied, because of COVID we are on duty and decided to assist your doctor. I looked to my doctor who, by the way, appeared to be quite young-looking and asked him are you sure this is routine and he smiled and reassured me it is a routine procedure. I then looked at my anesthesiologist and conveyed to him we are now besties and I need an extra helping of the sleepy, happy drug because I have been through the wash cycle and will be going through many more wash cycles! He smiled and said, "I've got you covered." This surgical experience prepared me well for the days and months ahead as it provided me with the human touch and reconfirmed although the COVID pandemic is trying to take control, we as humans still have compassion for each other.

As promised on May 1, 2020, there was a chemo chair with my name on it, a journey that requires a chapter of its own! Through all of this, my husband stood by my side, what a lucky girl I am; of course, the strong girl and the fixer in me of all problems needed to take control, so I tried my hardest to make him abandon me. Honestly, I did not want to feel guilty for the pain and agony I was going to impart on him and what if I died, how will he be able to move forward with all of my baggage he had to carry while I was undergoing treatment. I learned love is unconditional and does not have burdensome baggage. His love for me was not that of the schoolboy who fell for the pretty girl from a distance, it was that of my husband and father of our children. I am his soulmate and not a casual ornament on his arm, why could I not see this?

Well, I inadvertently and unknowingly allowed myself to be drained from all of those who had their objective for their world of success. You see, I was in a world where I did not belong, I was surrounded by the "wannabes." I thought I was helping them to be strong and successful because their peers were not kind to them. Little did I know their agenda was not in my best interest. They viewed me as part of their antagonizers and they intended to drain and discard me of all of my goodness. It took me a minute to figure out some folks don't mean you harm but will take advantage of opportunities that will place the royal crown on their head from my sweat, tears, and blood. For me, I was looking for a safe haven and figured the "wannabes" would be kind and fair to me, not wanting anything from me.

Quite frankly, it is up to me to protect myself and to stop waiting for someone to praise my work or character without a hidden motive. Hence, my husband is a good guy who has been trying to protect me for decades from the bullies who lured me in because I wanted to help them. I realized blame for that action is a two-way street and I am partially at fault, equipped with the vision to see the truth but refusing to do so. Honestly, though, sometimes we close our eyes or pretend what is there is not so, thereby, we align ourselves for the uncertain. I tried so hard to insight anger in my husband so that he would leave the parking lot and pick me up when I was ready. I knew he was in the car worried, praying, and wondering how could he take this away from me or take my place. I did not want him to feel melancholy or see the uncomfortable setting of cancer, so I pretended but when my legs could not pretend any longer, I reached for his hand which was always extended since the day we met as children! True love is not blind or selfish, it is deep with emotion and protection for the one you love. You know you are connected as soul mates when words are unnecessary to finish your sentence!

Chapter 6
Round 1 The Start of Chemo

The not as expected, or shall we say prognosticated pathology report that moved a forecasted Stage 0 to now Stage 3A cancer caused much chaos. This meant the prescribed treatment of possible radiation developed and spiraled into a chemo chair with my name on it less than a month after my surgery. Of course, my "cancer warriors" i.e., survivors who reached out to me from various encounters which I describe as encounters from God to humanly guide me through my cancer walk. My cancer warriors each played a significant role in my walk and will be referred to by their first name.

Ms. Anastacia, my son's teacher was the first to pave the way toward me, accepting my illness and knowing I will have to ask for help. The help needed here was to convey my illness just in case my will and strength to fight this disease was challenged, so she began to assemble a support channel for me.

Jayden, my son begins to retract into his man-made cave of protection. I needed Jayden to complete the school year and to know his mom will be okay. To my surprise, when I conveyed to Ms. Anastacia my illness, she conveyed her childhood illness and told me there was someone who could be of support to me during my cancer walk. I was connected to Shannon; I refer to her as the fearless lady warrior of our bunch because she went through the wringer with her cancer. Shannon answered all of my fact-finding questions regarding what to expect from chemo and how to prepare for my first treatment.

May 1, 2020, First Chemo Treatment: Of course, on the first day of chemo, I must be packed and equipped with all necessities for treatment. I packed my designer bag with the following contents: my daughter's favorite cartoon blanket to cover my arms and legs as if I was holding her in my arms, a liter of bottled water to stay hydrated, gum for dry mouth, a book to read, headphones for my phone and the most precious gift worn on my left wrist; a butterfly bracelet my son bought for me while we were on vacation at Dollywood. I also included a full set of change of clothes in case I became ill. I knew my husband was waiting for me in the car so I texted him while I was in the chemo chair and stated we will beat this. Naturally, I was nicely attired casually with my shoulder-length, perfectly angled, curly, silky, black hair which I snatched up in a ponytail to prepare for the infusion. I drank the liter of water because this would help me to flush out the poison being pumped into my body much faster. The only result from that action was me going to the bathroom right after my treatment several times and detesting the sight of bottled water to this day. I have to pour only lemon enhancers into my bottled water before I can consume it. My attending nurse was the head nurse in charge of helping out for the day. Her name was Nurse M., she was so patient with me and explained the procedure every step of the way. The different filled bags of clear liquids and their duration time along with the red bag of chemo med which would be the last drug to hang on the administering pole. Looking at the red bag of chemo med has caused me to refuse to drink anything red to this very day! My total infusion time was three hours, I had to weigh in for my fight, give blood through my new chemo port, wait until the blood results were reviewed by my doctor then I met with Dr. F briefly before the infusion began.

I thought I was in control of this day! How bad could chemo be? After all, you are sitting in a reclining chair relaxing for three and a half hours.

In the beginning, I referred to my chemo treatments as a chemo spa day, little did I know my intent to psychologically accept my situation and to allow myself to grieve would be anything but a chemo spa day! I wanted to be a better person after this experience, I did not want to suppress my pain as I did when my parents and sister died. When they passed on, I became robotic, outshining my own professional and personal records, working non-stop hours in high-level managerial positions, raising small children, being a wife, sister to my younger brother, and fixer/advisor for the world! Needless to say, I realized my behavior was not realistic and a severe burnout crash would occur, when I did not know but it was coming. I did not want the crash to occur after I beat cancer or during. So instead, I became human and grieved because my body was transforming quickly. I was battling for my life and existence on this earth. How could I inflict the same pain of death on my kids as I experienced from the passing of my parents? Who would help them through this pain? And, my poor husband, he can't prepare funny face pancakes for our kids and cut pineapple-shaped flowers and trees decorating and embellishing with other fruits to create a garden or forest. He will not press their clothes and hang them in the closet according to season. I can't die! There needs to be several fresh bouquets of flowers in our home weekly. My husband can't do this as this is my task. So, I sit in the chemo chair thinking of these things with a solution, *I must be a strong girl.* In my mind, my first chemo session needed to be successful as I had seven more to go. I conveyed this to Nurse M. When she stated with chemo hair loss will occur, I responded, "I will be in the category of those who do not lose their hair." She looked at me perplexed and gently tried to get me to accept the possibility. *I am a strong girl, if I will it, it will occur!*

The final ding from the chemo machine meant I completed my first session, Nurse M. needed to move a bit faster as I have to go in both senses of the phrase.

May 15, 2020 – Second Chemo Treatment and Son's Birthday: This treatment was one of my hardest as reality set in that this is not a 3.5-hour spa day; but rather, a battle for my life. I am very ladylike in my appearance meaning I always try to maintain a presentable appearance even if it is casual. On Sunday, May 10, I washed my hair with baby shampoo as one of my cancer survivors, Zenus, suggested as a tip. I made sure my curls were perfectly aligned but to my surprise, for the next four days, my scalp was burning as if a match was lit and burning on top of it. I did not take notice of this as I had to ensure my energy level and ebullience is present on May 15, since this is my son's birthday. As a mom, it was very important to me I did not switch roles and become the child in need of care and my child became the parent. Again, we were in the height of COVID so stay-at-home restrictions were in place, but how do you not celebrate the day God blessed me with a force of joy and love. I surreptitiously enlisted the aid of my sister-in-law to decorate our deck so that we can host an informal birthday party with a guest list that includes his siblings and parents. I recall purchasing two cakes because, for his first birthday, I was hospitalized for a non-life-threatening illness. I made a promise to him from that point onwards we would always celebrate his birthday with two cakes. Now, I am suffering from cancer and thinking why is this happening. Infusion day was filled with apprehension as I was beginning to exhibit a few of the side effects of which a copious amount of medication was prescribed to ward the illnesses off before the side effects make their presence known. My sense of smell was heightening and I was developing sensitivity and visual dislike for things associated with chemo. One would think these new developments would be enough.

However, this was not the reason for classifying this treatment as being one of the worst. After chemo and feeling prodigiously tired, I also felt my scalp burning uncontrollably, but I did not pay much attention to this as I needed to sit up straight and find a source of energy to wish my son a happy birthday and to ensure he had two cakes. My son had a nice, quiet birthday barbecue celebration concluding with the cutting of two cakes. That evening, I noticed my scalp burning and an unusual amount of hair in my brush. I noticed chunks of my hair coming out from the root. I could not process this because it was too soon. For the entire day, my hair was coming out with a strong force. I prayed and asked God for strength and to show me how to deal with whatever is occurring. The next day, I woke up and my hair was tangled as if I had dreadlocks. This was new to me as my hair was never in this state. It could not be brushed because of the tangles. I could not foresee or decipher this plan but I did desist from brushing my hair. I asked my husband to help me to cut out the tangles/dreads and he did with such care and ease. By the time he was done, I had strands of hair that were coming out when brushed. Within two days, I lost all of my hair with tiny strands remaining, this was devastating to me especially since I looked in the mirror and could still see a little bit of me! My husband shaved his hair and said, "We are in this together." I smiled with gratitude and fear as I did not know what was going on. My son could not look at me as my home was in turmoil because the reality of mom being ill with a life-threatening disease is now real. I recall not sleeping and walking downstairs to the kitchen when I saw my son at 3 am. I tried to get him to look at me because he didn't acknowledge me so we circled the kitchen island while his head was down. I was determined for him to look at me so that we can move forward to whatever steps are next.

I recall walking around our center kitchen island in a manner of cornering him, by the third walk around the island, he looked at me and said, "Why is this happening to you?" I knew exactly what he meant, my son always referred to me as too sweet and kind, so his words meant how something so horrible could be happening to a good person, my mom. I recall swallowing and holding back the tears because at this moment, I needed to say something profound to help my son and I needed those words to be filled with hope and not despair. I told him, "You are never given more than you can handle." I further conveyed how proud I am to be his mom and there is nothing in this world that would cause me to give up this role. He finally looked at me and our eyes locked. Of course, as I walked upstairs, I cried inside quietly while tears fell down my face. I knew I had to stay strong not only for me but for my family. Each of them was handling my illness differently but whatever the course of action, we had to remain strong and positive but realistic.

Yes, I am now bald and trying my hardest to wear hats, scarves, and a chemo cap. I called for a fitting of a wig since that appears to be the next step, but I sat down and thought about what was best for me. I did not want a wig, I wanted to beat cancer and this new person is someone that I do not know but I need to let her know it will be okay. When I reference the loss of my hair and the emotions associated with the loss, it is based on the normalcy of my life and not vanity. My son is accustomed to seeing his mom attired nicely in the morning to drop him off at school then off to work. He has never seen an emaciated, sick, bald lady who can barely stand up straight.

My third and fourth treatments had much anxiety before treatments and thereafter, I felt so tired and had no appetite. I ate my dinner on a small saucer. Dr. M stayed by my side just as he promised, he texted and called me multiple times before and after chemo to ensure I was doing okay. He saved me from being admitted to the hospital. I was enduring a side effect that was spiraling into a serious condition, Dr. M foresaw this condition coming and prescribed a medication which brought instant relief from this side effect. My sense of smell was so keen I could smell everything and most smells were not pleasant to me. I could smell the chemo center while at home and associated that smell with my treatments.

Chapter 7
Round 2 of Chemo

While undergoing chemo, you see faces of other patients which you remember, the one face I recall is Denise's. I recall Denise walking through the center for her treatment with the most beautiful short, curly hair and I thought that is how my hair might look. I also recall her confident walk and positive smile. When Denise and I spoke, I listened to her story then shared mine and realized we are all in the same situation with different scenarios. I recall telling Denise the names of my chemo drugs and she responded, "You are receiving the big guns meaning the potent drugs." My next round of chemo involved the use of Taxol which I referred to as liquid slow death. Why? This drug debilitated my body with no in-between recovery to prepare for the next session. I recall being told my first session was going to last for 4.5 hours right before the infusion. I basically freaked out! I was given Benadryl which caused me to react in a shaking manner then Taxol was infused with a reaction of continued shaking and uneasiness. My nurse noticed my uncontrollable shaking and inability to stay calm and conveyed to me she thinks I am experiencing an allergic reaction. I recall looking at the clock and thinking I cannot do this! I requested to speak with the counselor onsite. Mark, the counselor, introduced himself and sat with me talking for over an hour which was so helpful to me as I needed that diversion from shaking. This treatment was brutal as it made me weak and compromised my ability to stand and walk. I would always go to the restroom after the infusion needle was removed from my chemo port. However, I noticed Round 2's sessions were not only debilitating but my brain was being taken hostage from the medication. I recall counting the steps to the restroom from my infusion chair. I further did a full assessment of the restroom since it was a private restroom only to be used by one person. Meaning, I counted the steps to the sink and the toilet as I could not digest falling near the toilet in a compromising position, so I developed a system of cold water on my face, timing myself in between the alertness of the cold water to returning to my dizzy and confused state. I prayed not to fall in the restroom, I prayed the nurses would not detect I was not strong enough to maneuver on my own, and most of all I prayed for my infusion to end with me walking out of the center and not experience a spasm in my legs.

I had four treatments of Taxol and each treatment debilitated me a bit more than the former treatment. My fingers and toes were in pain from neuropathy and nothing I used would alleviate this pain. I went into my medicine cabinet locating every massage oil, lotion, etc. that I thought would help me. I found a bottle of CBD oil that my acupuncturist sold to me a while ago. I never knew what this oil was made from as I thought it was an all-natural herbal oil. I used the CBD oil and received immediate relief then I researched its chemical components, paused for a moment in thought, and realized I am in pain and I need this help. Preparing for the steps of treatment, I sought as much support and information as I could for not only myself but my family specifically my son. I recall my counselor offering me a prescription for medicinal marijuana and I shunned the offer. I never used any kind of drugs, smoked, or drank but I tell you when you are experiencing unimaginable pain you will be grateful for whatever help or medication is available. I can only speak for me but the CBD oil truly lessened my pain and I was actually able to move my fingers and hold my teacup.

Taxol is not an easy drug as it really debilitated me. I could not walk without dropping to my knees from spasms. I could barely climb up and down the stairs. Needless to say, the last round of chemo was acrimonious but I knew I had to be strong and withstand all of the side effects. It was so difficult, Dr. F offered me the opportunity to forgo my last treatment. I declined his offer and went for it, that treatment felt as though Mike Tyson, Ali, and Sugar Ray Leonard beat me to a pulp. I was in so much pain, if you looked at me that was painful! I am glad I subjected myself to the last treatment because I would have wondered if the next step to this journey was a lack of me not taking the last infusion. After my first surgery in April, the pathology report showed evidence of cancer remaining; thereby, I would eventually have to endure a mastectomy. During chemo, I kept praying for a miracle that would result in me not having to undergo a mastectomy. However, my doctor burst that bubble prayer into a reality of now you must schedule surgery with Dr. H's office. I was flabbergasted and disappointed as I thought and hoped chemo would cure me. That did not occur.

Before undergoing surgery on September 8, 2020, my surgeon ordered a mammogram to see the effects of chemo, I thought maybe this is my chance to be cured and not undergo surgery again and to be cancer-free. Well, the mammogram showed calcification forming meaning cancer may be returning. I was so heartbroken but I took a deep breath and asked the attending doctor who reviewed my mammogram results, if it was her what would she do? She responded, "Go through with the mastectomy." I thought about what she said for a minute and responded, "Yes, I will go for the mastectomy because the very part of me that I am trying to save is now an enemy trying to take my life."

Chapter 8
Saying Good-Bye

I was allowed one month of rest from chemo to prepare for my surgery. This was not easy as I thought about how I will regain my strength and if I do not, then there may be a delay in my surgery. I cannot allow any of this to occur especially since it appeared as though something was reforming in me. I rested and was not fearful at all of the surgery even when I learned I have no options remaining. Of course, weight loss for me was a concern because the loss of weight played a role in my physical strength which was diminishing. I weighed myself almost every day and forced lots of protein down my throat along with supplements. My appetite was non-existent but I knew I had to eat to make it through surgery. I looked through my lingerie drawer and wondered if I would ever wear any of my bras again. Then I realized there may be a new me but how much newer me can I handle. All through my treatments, I would glance in the mirror and I noticed the person looking back at me is a stranger. I do not know her; would I ever be able to live with this new me and what kind of path or choices would I make moving forward? I always knew my responsibilities and I chose my path based on what was expected of me. Now, I have a chance to become the person I could have become and to make my own choices, this was scary to think of and to do!

A week before my surgery, my littlest one sat in my lap in the very chair I rocked her to sleep when she was a wee one and asked me about my cut. My cut was my reference point to my surgery in a language not too descriptive when she and I discussed why I could not hug or hold her. Her question about my cut placed an uncomfortable feeling in my heart, so much so, I began to evaluate my health and situation.

My son even questioned me about this surgery, so now I have two kids inquiring. This was not a comforting feeling as it brought uneasiness to me. The night before my surgery I kissed my son and told him to attend school online and not to worry about me as I will be fine. I also told him if he did not feel mentally up to attending school, I will understand and leave that decision to him. As I proceeded to move along to the next bedroom, I engaged in a conversation with my "Shadow." I call her Shadow because she follows me around and mimics my exact behavior, this is so uncanny! She and I chatted, during our conversation, I felt the strong urge to tell her no matter what I want her to achieve her dreams and be as you are intended to be and do in this world. She looked at me and said, "That will only happen if you live." I took a deep breath and realized she knew exactly what I was doing. I was saying "Good-bye" to her because I did not want her last memory to be of confusion. I knew that she was smart enough to remember our conversation and know that I wanted her to carry on. I walked back to my bedroom with tears in my eyes, crying and kneeling and asking God to guide me through my surgery with profound success and to spare my life because I am needed by my kids and I need them!

Surgery day, my husband informed me he was not leaving the parking lot. He walked me into the entry of the hospital since that was as far as he could escort me. My surgery was scheduled for 7:30 am. I had to report to the hospital at 5:30 am. It was a ghost town. I remember praying my legs would not give out on me and those painful spasms would not make an appearance until I am in the company of medical professionals and not in a corridor. Out of nowhere came this wonderful hospital employee, who escorted me to the nurse's station. My surgery lasted for three hours; I recall the anesthesiologist introducing herself, and then I recall feeling a bit woozy. I asked her did she give me some happy medicine and she responded, "Yes, I did." She assured me all will be well and they will take good care of me. I met all of the surgical team and my surgeon visited me before surgery, we laughed, and then I knew God was reassuring me I was not going into the operating room alone.

I recall waking up at noon after my three-hour surgery with the most wonderful nurse at my side. She informed me my room was not ready since my condition warrants me to be in a room by myself and the hospital is on high COVID alert. Well, 6:00 pm rolled around and I was still in recovery, it was time for her to leave for the day but she refused and told me she will not leave until I am in a room. I was moved into my room at 6:05 pm and I found out the nurse's persistence in checking on my room availability was one of the reasons for the move. My surgeon even visited me after I awoke from the procedure and I further recall one of the doctors helping me up so that he could further wrap my wound. I was so fortunate now that I am looking back at the care and attention I received from surgery. I was admitted into the hospital for two days since my recovery was very slow the first day. Meaning, I was not eating and my nurse was in the process of placing me back on an IV. I recall one of my nurses telling me I have to try to get up and walk. She promised she would walk with me and told me not to worry, I will be fine just keep trying to eat something no matter how little it is. My appetite was completely gone and I wanted nothing to eat, but the thought of the IV in my arm was enough to make me nibble. Eating was never a high priority for me just as balancing work and life was a foreign concept to me, but I realized if I do not change my life to include a healthy lifestyle amalgamated with rest and peacefulness, I may not exist for much longer.

Chapter 9
Healing and Recuperating

Now that I have undergone a mastectomy and part of me is gone, this pathology report was much better than the first. Meaning, only one lymph node was infected with cancer and there was cancer found within the inner walls which means radiation will or should eradicate any cancer in the bed of my chest as I understand it from the intricate medical elucidation. I was assigned a couple of nurses to care for me at home while I am recuperating, that is, to change my dressing and an occupational therapist to help me with mobility. During my recuperation, I noticed my stomach swelling which meant the movement of protein from the lymph nodes needed assistance i.e., therapeutic massages, etc. All of this is new to me and a bit intimidating. I was frightened this was a means of cancer traveling, I know that sounds silly but after going through as much as I have gone through in such a short time, the mind tends to wander into an avenue of nonsense. While recuperating, I discovered from the observations of my nurses how much my illness has affected my husband. He was grieving for me. He changed my dressing and took such good care of me.

However, after I began to heal one of my nurses asked me why am I wearing the wrap around my chest and she indicated it was not necessary, but I thought it was because it brought me comfort. Well, I decided on a Friday to remove the wrap and I looked at my chest and began to cry for three days because a part of me was gone and I could not understand "Why?" I allowed myself to be sad and I prayed for strength to accept the new me. I took a deep breath and said to myself, "You are alive but do not settle for just living, instead, the quality of your life needs to ameliorate immensely." The next step in my healing was to purchase a compression bra, of course, amid COVID I researched and ordered every bra I could find to no avail. My husband decided to take me on what I refer to as a "human ride" which was a long car ride anywhere. As we passed over a bridge, I noticed an outlet mall and told him I have to find a workable bra, perhaps the sports store might have one that will work. I had no energy to shop or to walk and of course, my husband did not want me to leave the car but I knew I needed to hold on to my dignity and find my bra. I got out of the car and passed the Kate Spade store. I love purses and have a closet full of them as they make me happy. I went into the store and felt absolutely nothing as I was dead inside. I was the only customer and I heard this mellifluous voice complimenting me on the blue chemo cap that I was wearing. I responded, "Thank you" in an oblivious tone then she complimented me on my shoe which were UGG's sandals that I wore with socks because of the neuropathy in my foot. I then stopped and thought she must have a strange sense of style, then I looked at my reflection in the mirror which was a fragile, bald woman in pain.

The salesperson was behind the counter and I asked her a random question then it all made sense, she was reaching out to me because she too was a cancer survivor. She detected the lost look in my eyes and wanted to connect with me. When she revealed her story to me, and I asked her did she recognize me as being in our cancer sorority, she smiled and said, "Yes." I thanked her because she woke me up from my daze. I told her I needed to purchase a bra and I don't know what to do. She suggested that I should go to the Nike store and conveyed it will be okay. She told me not only is she fighting her battle with cancer but so is her mom. I told her every encounter happens for a reason. I thanked her for her compliments even if they were spurious, she woke me up to my reality. We never exchanged names or contact information but she told me we will see each other again; I could not understand that but she further indicated our meeting was faith and the Lord's work because healing comes in multiple levels.

My husband and I began to head home since I was successful in purchasing my sports bras. I turned on *I Don't Wanna* by Toni Braxton and told him to listen to the words because that is how I feel. I saw the attentiveness in his eyes as the song played listening to the words. When the song concluded, he took a deep breath and said, "Wow, I had no idea."

I told him I have a collection of songs that I listened to while undergoing chemo but this one expresses my feelings the best. He and I did not have many words to exchange but there was a sense of completion. He and I would set aside time to take human rides as it would re-energize us. There were rides when I would endure pain-stacking spasms from sitting for a while, then there were rides when I would sleep through. I realized how much I needed my husband's love, support, and hopeful spirit for my recovery. Fighting cancer is hard but doing it alone is just as hard. You have to remember whatever your situation, you must acknowledge the hurt of your situation travels from you to your supporters. My husband remained calm and patient especially during the days when I was irritated because I could not follow our full conversation. Yes, chemo does tamper with your mental ability to think logically and recall some details within a conversation.

Chapter 10
My Body Has Been Cut, Poisoned, Chopped, and Now Burned!

Now that I have recuperated from surgery with an acceptance of my new body, the next step is radiation. This does not sound too bad, how bad can it be compared to chemo? Well, if eight lymph nodes are removed from your arm and you just had surgery, this is not a piece of cake. I had to endure 28 sessions of radiation during COVID. What does that mean? I could not change into the gown at the center, instead, I had to put on the oversized, green half gown that was always missing the inside strap while at home before entering the center for treatment. I felt like a piece of meat when I laid on the table. I lost a piece of my dignity each session. This experience was not one of comfortability, I do strongly believe receiving radiation during COVID removed the human factor and replaced it with robotic-ness and a system of measurement, or should I say quota for the day. The staff tried their best to be friendly and reassuring, but at the end of the day, feeling the intensity of COVID precautions and dealing with cancer was too much to tolerate mentally. I felt less of a human being each time I tried to engage in general conversation, only to be looked at with visual conveyance of "We need you to hurry up and put on your top so that the next patient can receive his/her treatment." I was undergoing preventive lymphedema treatment while undergoing radiation and I can honestly say, my therapist, Melissa is an angel sent from God to help me through my treatment. I was badly burned and she patiently helped me with wound care and keeping my burned limps comfortably while massaging my arm.

During my fourth week of treatment, my skin began to peel down to the tissue as I recall. I was in so much pain, and of course, this was around Christmas! I was in so much pain, tears could not even flow from my eyes, none of the pain meds worked because my body was immune to most of the prescription pain meds. Again, my only hope during that dark time was Melissa and her treatment – mostly wound care. My husband had to change my dressing and I am not sure how he did it without breaking down, it was pretty bad and not pleasant to look at if you are not familiar with burn cases. I do feel pretty lucky though because my chest area peeled but not down to the white tissue part. Of course, I could not complete the two remaining radiation treatments but at least I was able to complete 26 treatments, believe me, I prayed hard each day for my skin to withstand the burns and for me to be able to remain in the uncomfortable, over the head position. I am very fortunate and as a Catholic, I can say, the power of God was with me every step of the way! I was not officially diagnosed with lymphedema as we are in the preventive stage, I am hopeful I will prevail in this area. I am very fortunate my journey on the cancer road resulted in an assembly of competent doctors, the best in their area of specialty, nurses whose compassion was outstanding, therapists whose knowledge is underestimated by their humbleness and unspoken excellence, new cancer survivor friends who understand what is spoken with the use of minimal words, colleagues who have become family, strangers who extended an automatic prayer for my survival and last but never the least, my family who never gave up on me surviving, especially my husband. Well, now you have heard my story, and believe me, it is a journey I would not wish on anyone. I know how fortunate I am to have been given a second chance, that is why no day of my life will be taken for granted. I have my bad days and good days, but through it all, I know each day is a blessing!

Chapter 11
Acknowledgment and
Thank You

Cancer Medical Team: On my journey or cancer walk, my medical team equipped me with the following:

Lead Doctors: I refer to my three lead doctors as my wise medical men.

- Dr. Firozi brought the truth to my condition. You have cancer.
- Dr. Habibi brought strength when my knees were buckling after chemo. He restored my fight.
- Dr. Muttath brought forgiveness to thy self and others. I would not have survived my chemo treatment without Dr. Muttath, he checked in with me almost daily during the four months of chemo, then weekly thereafter. He promised to walk this road with me and kept his word! He even called me to gauge my mental spirit during chemo.

Medical Specialist:

- Dr. Tarver helped me to connect to my faith, and not be afraid to pray and ask for help. She is truly a phenomenal lady whose style and brilliance are admirable.
- Dr. Levenson's quick action and compassion helped to lead me to the beginning of my cancer journey and saved my life. If she had dismissed my situation as nothing, I would not be alive!
- Dr. Lee's compassion and kindness helped me to tolerate radiation and to know I will survive.

CPSIA information can be obtained
at www.ICGtesting.com
Printed in the USA
LVHW050134281222
735870LV00012B/353